Abby Flies a Kite

A Book about Wind

BY KERRY DINMONT

Published by The Child's World®
1980 Lookout Drive • Mankato, MN 56003-1705
800-599-READ • www.childsworld.com

Photographs ©: Photo Melon/Shutterstock Images, cover, 1 (top); Mike
Ledray/Shutterstock Images, 1 (bottom); Shutterstock Images, 3, 5,
10–11, 16–17; Sergey Novikov/Shutterstock Images, 6, 9, 13, 14, 21;
Dmitriy Sudzerovskiy/Shutterstock Images, 18

Design Elements: Mike Ledray/Shutterstock Images

ISBN 9781503820142
LCCN 2016960933

Printed in the United States of America
PA02339

Today, Abby flies a kite.

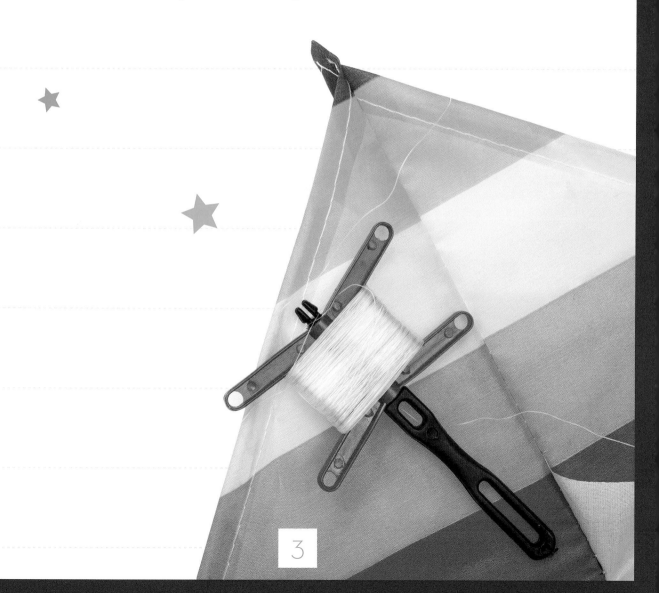

How does it fly?

It is windy. Abby takes her kite to a **field**.

Abby holds the **string**.

She starts to run.

The **wind** pushes down on the kite.

It crashes to the ground.

Next, Abby stands still.

Her back is to the wind.

She holds the kite high.

14

Abby lets go of the kite.

She holds the string.

The wind pushes the

kite up and away.

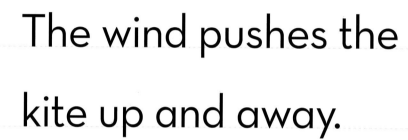

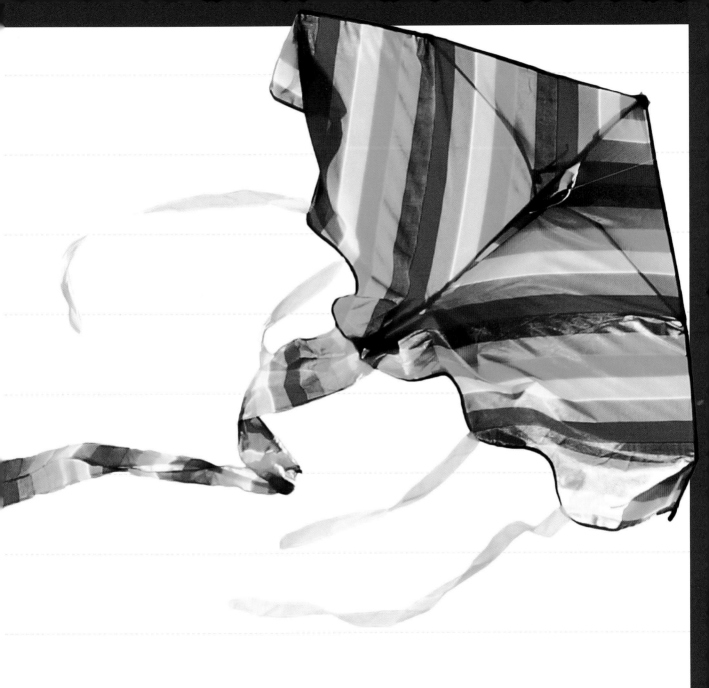

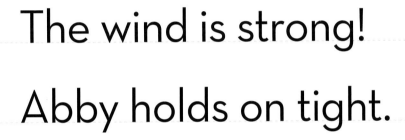

The wind is strong!

Abby holds on tight.

Have you ever flown a kite?

21

Words to Know

field (FEELD) A field is a large piece of open land. A field is a great place to fly a kite.

string (STRING) A string is a thin rope. Abby holds tight to the string when she flies her kite.

wind (WIND) Wind is moving air. Wind is what makes kites fly.

Extended Learning Activities

1 When was the last time you flew a kite? How did you get the kite to fly?

2 Kites come in many shapes and colors. What does your favorite kite look like?

3 What makes a field a good place to fly a kite?

To Learn More

Books

Benduhn, Tea. *Wind Power*. Pleasantville, NY: Weekly Reader, 2009.

Lowery, Lawrence F. *How Does the Wind Blow?*
New York, NY: Holt, Rinehart and Winston, 2013.

Web Sites

Visit our Web site for links about wind:
childsworld.com/links

Note to Parents, Teachers, and Librarians: We routinely verify our Web links to make sure they are safe and active sites. So encourage your readers to check them out!

About the Author

Kerry Dinmont is a children's book author who enjoys art and nature. She lives in Montana with her two Norwegian elkhounds.